WOW!
Oceans

A Book of Extraordinary Facts

KINGFISHER

First published 2019 by Kingfisher
an imprint of Macmillan Children's Books
The Smithson, 6-9 Briset Street, London EC1M 5NR
Associated companies throughout the world
www.panmacmillan.com

Author and consultant: Camilla de la Bédoyère
Design and styling: Liz Adcock
Jacket design: Liz Adcock
Illustrations: Ste Johnson

ISBN 978-0-7534-4480-1

1 3 5 7 9 8 6 4 2
1TR/0719/WKT/UG/140WFO

A CIP catalogue record for this book is available from the British Library.

Printed in China

WOW!
Oceans

A Book of Extraordinary Facts

KINGFISHER

Oceans are BIG!

All five oceans, and about 20 seas, are connected to each other and create the World Ocean.

There are five huge areas of salty water on the planet. They are called oceans and together they cover 70 per cent of the Earth's surface. That's why we call our home the Blue Planet!

Atlantic Ocean

I'm a giant squid.

I'm an ocean sunfish.

Sailing all around the world takes at least 40 days!

Pacific Ocean

Wow!

Salty water makes a great home for animals. The largest squid are bigger than a bus, but the smallest ones are tinier than your thumbnail!

4

I'm a walrus.

Arctic Ocean

Guess what?

There are vast mountains and volcanoes beneath the seas. Some are so deep in places that even Mount Everest – the tallest mountain on land – would disappear beneath the surface!

The oceans hold about 679,000,000,000,000 bathtubs full of salty water. That's 679 trillion!

Pacific Ocean

Indian Ocean

We are clown fish.

Whose tail is this?

Southern Ocean

I'm a king penguin.

5

Focus on fish

The oceans are a home for billions of fish, which come in all shapes and sizes!

Butterfly fish look like butterflies, parrot fish have beak-like mouths and pineapple fish look like pineapples!

which do you think I am?

I'm an **oarfish** and I'm **reallllly long!**

An oarfish looks like a long, silvery ribbon and measures up to 15 metres long!

Wow!

Many fish use venom to sting their prey, or to defend themselves. Electric fish have a different super power – they zap other animals with a big electric shock!

Thwack!

Titan triggerfish don't like people! If something or someone gets too close to a titan triggerfish, they may get bitten or walloped by a mighty tail.

oww!

Freaky-looking frogfish open up their giant mouth and suck in their prey faster than a vacuum cleaner!

we're in a big school!

I'm cleaning up!

Wow!

A big group of fish is called a school or shoal, and swimming together helps fish to avoid attacks from hungry predators. A single school of silvery herring can contain more than 10 million fish!

Long-distance swimmers

Travel through the oceans with these awesome explorers.

There's a great reward in store for a hungry grey whale. This big beast swims 8000 kilometres to reach the Arctic Sea, where it feasts on 70 tonnes of food during the summer!

Where's my dinner?

Slow down, kids!

Blue shark mums swim across the Atlantic Ocean before giving birth to up to 50 babies!

Wow!

Spiny lobsters hold onto each other as they march across the seabed in a long line!

A long animal journey is called a migration. Animals migrate to find food or mates, or safe places to have their young. The world's longest migrations all take place at sea.

Slow and steady wins the race!

One record-breaking leatherback turtle swam an incredible 20,557 kilometres across the world's oceans.

Are we nearly there yet?

Eels trek an epic 5000 kilometres across the Atlantic Ocean. They swim the whole way without eating or resting!

Left, right! Left, right! 9

Dive into the forest

Join super-cute sea otters in a lush green paradise. But watch out for what's lurking underneath...

There are huge forests growing under the water. Made of giant kelp, these forests are home to many animals, including sea otters.

I'm a **Sea urchin** and I eat the **kelp** - **yum!**

Wow!

A single kelp plant can be 65 metres long, and it grows up to 45 centimetres a day! Kelp is seaweed, or algae, which is a type of plant that grows in salty water.

I'm a **Sea otter** and I eat **sea urchins!**

Algae and other sea plants help our planet's health by making oxygen. It's the gas that humans and other animals need to breathe to stay alive!

I'm fishing for fry!

In warm places, where the land meets the sea, mangrove trees grow. Their long roots make a perfect hiding place for crocodiles and other animals.

Baby fish are called fry.

We're hiding from scary crocs!

Wow!

Sea beasts called dugongs and manatees live near the shore, where they eat seagrasses. They pop their heads above water to breathe. People have mistaken them for mermaids!

Wonderful whales

These mighty mammals are clever, strong and precious.

The smallest whales are 1 metre-long dolphins and porpoises, but the largest are 33 times longer and 3000 times heavier!

I'm blowing my nose!

Danger!

A quarter of all types of whale and dolphin are in danger of dying out forever. In the past, humans hunted thousands of whales every year, but now most countries protect them.

Whales can stay underwater for more than an hour, but they come to the surface to breathe. The blowholes on top of their heads are nostrils!

Hello up there!

Whales and dolphins are clever animals that can talk to each other with deep booming calls, clicks or whistles.

Incredible killer whales are so clever they can plan attacks on their prey! They work in teams to knock seals off ice floating in the sea.

Surprise!

uh oh!

Wow!

Whales are mammals, which means they give birth to their babies and feed them with milk. Mothers teach their babies how to find food and stay safe.

Can you hear singing?

Hey mum, watch me spurt water from my blowhole!

Brrr... it's icy cold

Explore the mysterious icy oceans,
where it's so cold the sea freezes.

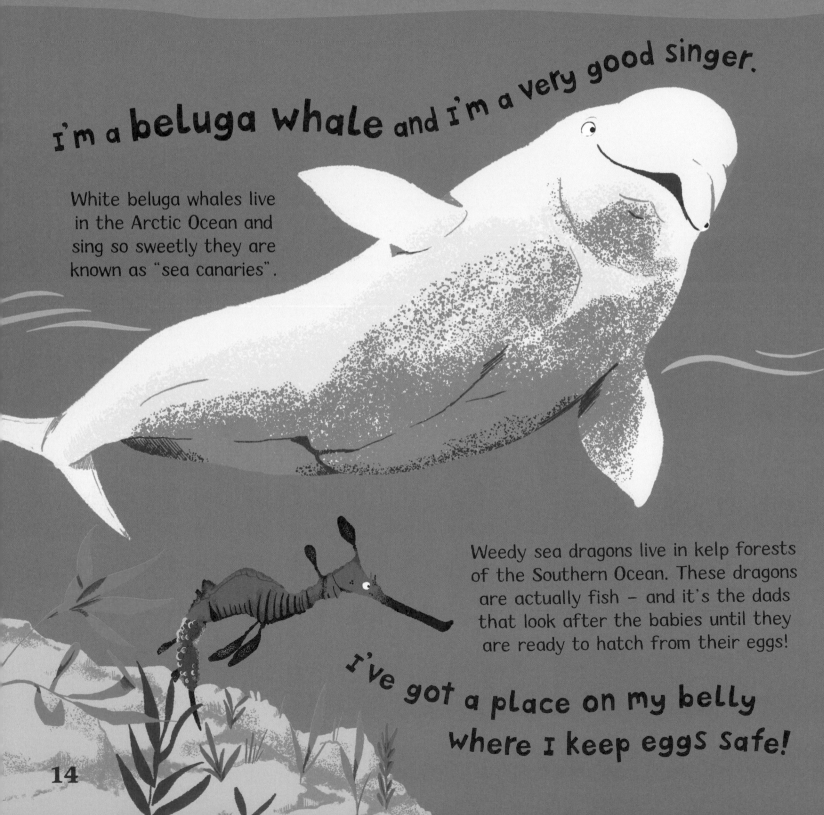

I'm a beluga whale and I'm a very good singer.

White beluga whales live
in the Arctic Ocean and
sing so sweetly they are
known as "sea canaries".

Weedy sea dragons live in kelp forests
of the Southern Ocean. These dragons
are actually fish – and it's the dads
that look after the babies until they
are ready to hatch from their eggs!

I've got a place on my belly
where I keep eggs safe!

Wow!

Sheets of ice form in the polar oceans. Mountains of ice, called icebergs, sometimes break away and float in the sea.

Eeeeek! Swim away!

I'm coming for you!

Polar bears are great swimmers, and deadly predators. They can hear a seal swimming one metre below thick ice!

I'm a narwhal. I can use my tooth to whack a fish.

The longest tooth in the world belongs to a male narwhal. He has only two teeth, but one of them can grow to 3 metres long. People used to think that narwhals' teeth came from unicorns!

Down to the deep

Are you scared of the dark? There are some strange animals in the inky-black deep sea.

Viperfish don't mind the dark because they can make their own light! They dangle a light in front of their face and swallow up curious fish that come to investigate.

Did you know?

Sunlight passes through sea water, and helps the plants that live there to grow. Below 1000 metres there is no light at all and the sea becomes a dark, cold and scary place.

I'm a viperfish. Here, fishy fishy!

I'm a giant isopod.

Giant isopods look like huge woodlice. They can grow to 35 centimetres long and use their long feelers to find their way in the dark.

Vampire squid have huge eyes and they can make their whole body shimmer with light to scare other animals away.

Ooh, I'm SO scary!

Wow!
If you tried to live in the deep sea, you'd find the weight of water above you is so great that you'd be crushed to pulp!

A gulper eel has such a big mouth it can swallow animals bigger than itself.

GULP!

In some places, hot water and gases escape from under the sea bed and bubble into the sea. Weird, freaky animals, like hairy-clawed yeti crabs, live in these hotspots!

snip snip!

17

Coral reefs

Did you know that coral reefs are big enough to be seen from space?

There's a carnival of colour in a coral reef! It makes a perfect home for billions of animals that find places to hide and hunt in the shadows.

I'm a regal angelfish.

I'm a porcupine fish.

I'm a blue tang.

We need sunlight and clean, salty water to grow.

Wow!

The Great Barrier Reef of Australia is actually a collection of about 3000 reefs and 1000 islands that are spread over 2000 kilometres in the Coral Sea. It's the largest living structure on Earth.

I'm a parrot fish.

I'm a seahorse.

I'm a mandarin fish.

Corals become different shapes and colours as they grow. Brain coral look like brains, fan corals look like fans and lettuce corals look like... can you guess?

Did you know?

A coral reef may be huge, but it's built by tiny animals that are no bigger than a fingernail! These animals are called polyps (say pol-IPs) and they build rocky cups to sit in.

Ocean giants

The seas are home to some super-sized animals. They can be super speedy too!

Blue whales are so big that a whole one has never been weighed. A blue whale's poo is pink and longer than a person!

I'm the biggest creature on Earth!

This creepy-crawly Japanese spider crab has very long legs. It measures 370 centimetres from one side to the other.

Big mouth!

The world's biggest fish is the gentle whale shark. It's so large you could sit in its mouth!

I can live to 100 years old!

Wow!

Have you noticed how easy it is to float in sea water? It's denser, or thicker, than fresh water and that means it can support heavy bodies like these ocean giants.

My tusks are still growing!

Weighty walruses lumber slowly on the ice, but they are sleek swimmers underwater. They use their huge tusks to pull themselves back on to ice or land.

"Eye" can see you! This colossal squid has huge eyes – each one is as big as a dinner plate!

open wide!

I'm a colossal squid
and I can grow to 10 metres long.

Giant clams live around coral reefs where there is so much food they can grow to be 1 metre wide, and can live for 100 years.

Meet the sharks

Great white sharks are fast, furious hunters – but not all sharks are scary!

This shortfin mako is the world's fastest shark, speeding through the water like a blue bullet at 80 kilometres an hour.

I'm super speedy!

Wow!

Shark skeletons are made of cartilage, which is a bit bendier than normal bone. Your nose and ears can bend because they have cartilage in them.

Wow!

Sharks' skin is covered in thousands of scales that are made of super-strong enamel – just like your teeth!

Humans? Yuk! No thanks!

Great whites are huge, fast and clever sharks that mostly hunt fish and seals. They don't really like the taste of humans... that's a relief!

Why do hammerheads have such weird heads? This strange shape works like an aeroplane wing, helping a hammerhead shark to change direction quickly.

I'm a hammerhead shark. I can see all around – even behind.

Get in my belly!

Basking sharks have huge mouths for gulping down lots of tiny sea creatures. They have 1500 teeth, but they are harmless to people.

Can you see me?

Wobbegong sharks are so well camouflaged among seaweed and stones that they can lie on the sea bed and just wait until a fish swims close by. Then it's snap, gobble, swallow!

23

Coastal capers

Not all ocean creatures live in the sea. Take a look at the animals who like life above the water.

Penguins surf...

Penguins waddle on land but they are sleek swimmers and surfers in the sea! They use the waves to help them leap on to land.

surf's up everyone - Let's play!

Wind power!

Waves are caused by wind. It whips up water at the top of the sea, turning it into a frothy white wave, especially at the coast.

Marine iguanas dive...

These reptiles live on land, but they swim to the sea bed where they nibble on seaweed.

Wake up! it's time for lunch!

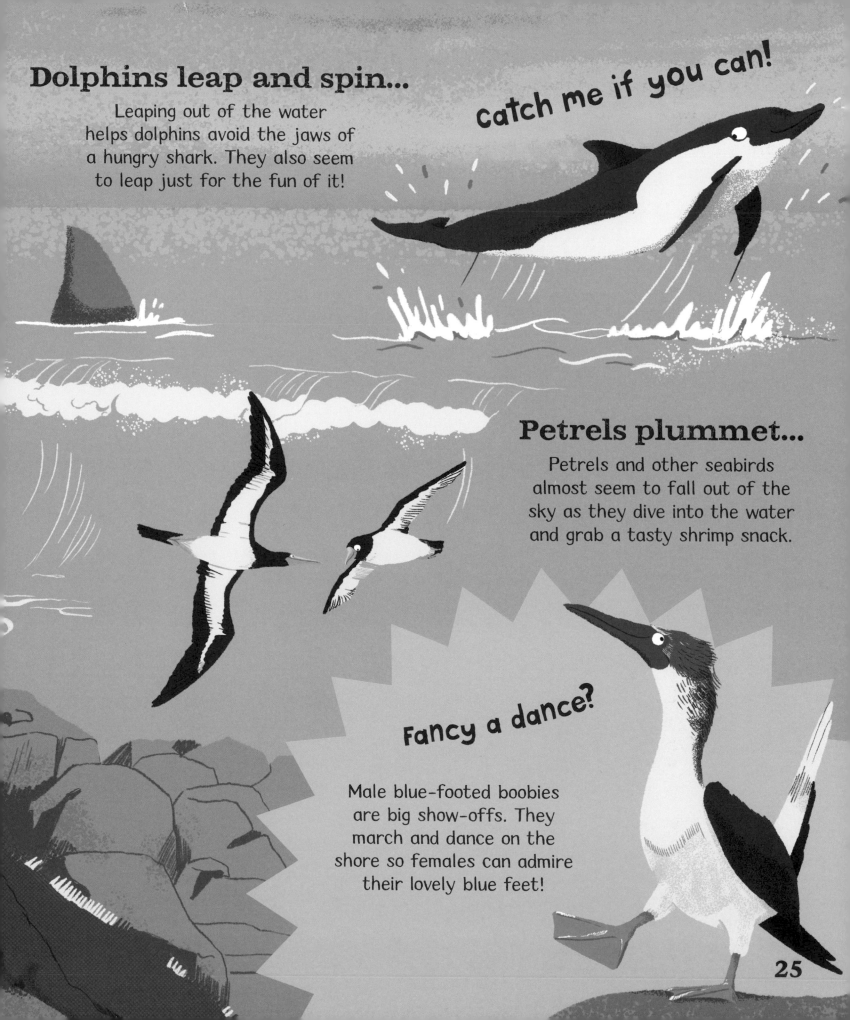

Dolphins leap and spin...

Leaping out of the water helps dolphins avoid the jaws of a hungry shark. They also seem to leap just for the fun of it!

Catch me if you can!

Petrels plummet...

Petrels and other seabirds almost seem to fall out of the sky as they dive into the water and grab a tasty shrimp snack.

Fancy a dance?

Male blue-footed boobies are big show-offs. They march and dance on the shore so females can admire their lovely blue feet!

Freaky sea creatures

Which is the strangest animal in the sea? You decide!

Burp!

Yuck!

Hagfish look like gross, slimy worms, but they have a toothy mouth that bites chunks of flesh from their victims. They even swim into another animal's mouth and eat it from the inside. That's revolting!

I'm a tentacled terror with super suckers!

A cuttlefish has eight arms for grabbing prey and two tentacles. It has three hearts that pump blue blood and it can change colour in a flash!

Munch crunch!

Most starfish have five arms, but a crown-of-thorns starfish can have 20! It nibbles at coral and has damaged large parts of the Great Barrier Reef.

26

The largest jellyfish are bigger than an adult, and they have long tentacles that are covered in nasty stingers.

I'm not a fish and I'm not made of jelly!

Wow!

Sea sponges don't have heads, hearts, eyes, legs, brains or even mouths – but they have been around for more than 600 million years!

SNIP SNAP!

Crabs like to arm wrestle! Males grow one huge claw that they use to wave at their enemies, and if the threat doesn't work, they fight instead.

Scary seas

Meet some ocean killers with special skills. Don't get too near these creatures!

A blue-ringed octopus is smaller than a tennis ball, but its venom is strong enough to kill a person.

I'm small but deadly!

Wow!

Venom is poison that an animal uses to kill or injure another animal. Many ocean animals use spines or teeth to inject their venom.

stay away!

Scary stonefish are difficult to see on the seabed, but they have venom in their 13 spines – and they can still sting once they are dead!

Roarrrr!

Lionfish look lovely with their colourful stripes – but they are crafty killers. When a lionfish is scared, it raises its spines and stabs an attacker with a nasty dose of venom.

Mantis shrimps can punch their prey with such force they can break glass, or kill a crab in less than a second.

I'm a mantis shrimp and I'm really strong!

Wow!

Seashells can look harmless, but nasty nippers can live inside! Cone shells fire a poisoned harpoon at their prey. The venom is deadly to people!

Slithering sea snakes have some of the deadliest venom in the world. Thankfully, they are shy and swim away from people.

SSSSSSSS!

Ocean adventure

There are lots of fun and exciting ways to explore the ocean!

Surfing is so much fun that some dogs like to do it too! If they fall off their boards, it's easy for dogs to get back to shore – they doggy paddle, of course!

Did you know?

Plastiki is a boat made of 12,500 plastic bottles! It was sailed from the United States of America to Australia to help people learn how plastic is damaging the ocean.

I must be barking mad to do this!

More people have been to the Moon than the deepest part of the ocean!

Humans explore the deep sea in special vessels called submersibles. In 1960, two men travelled more than 10,000 metres down. They were surprised to find some little red shrimp living there!

You can explore under the ocean waves using a snorkel or scuba gear. Snorkels are breathing tubes that connect your mouth to the air above, but scuba divers take tanks of air down with them.

Don't try this at home!

I use my hands to "talk" underwater.

Wow!

Freedivers swim deep without taking any air with them. They can hold their breath for more than 20 minutes, but it's a very dangerous sport!

The world's biggest cruise ship takes more than 5000 people on holiday. Once on board, they can enjoy 24 swimming pools, a giant slide, an ice rink and an open-air theatre!

Swim, slide, eat – repeat!

Save our seas!

Our beautiful oceans are in trouble. How can we help?

Lots of our plastic waste ends up in the oceans, where it damages the animals that live there.

Use less plastic, and ALWAYS recycle it!

Wow!

12 million tonnes of plastic get into the oceans every year. Turtles often mistake plastic bags for jellyfish and die when they try to eat them.

Let's go swimming!

Turtles lay their eggs on beaches and, once hatched, baby turtles crawl down to the sea. Beaches covered in litter make it very difficult for the baby turtles to find their way to the water.

We burn fossil fuels, such as oil and gas, to heat our homes and travel in cars – but that's making the oceans too warm.

I'm walking to school!

Going GREEN can SAVE our blue planet!